What is Murder?

Murder descends from the **Proto-Indo-European** *mŕ̥-trom* which meant "killing", a noun derived from *mer-* "to die".

Proto-Germanic in fact had two nouns derived from this word, later merging into the modern English noun: *murþrą* "death, killing, murder" (directly from Proto-Indo-European *mŕ̥-trom*), whence **Old English** *morðor* "secret or unlawful killing of a person, murder; mortal sin, crime; punishment, torment, misery";[and *murþrijô* "murderer; homicide" (from the verb *murþrijaną* "to murder"), giving Old English *myrþra* "homicide, murder; murderer". There was a third word for "murder" in Proto-Germanic, continuing Proto-Indo-European *mr̥tós* "dead" (compare Latin *mors*), giving Proto-Germanic *murþą* "death, killing, murder" and Old English *morþ* "death, crime, murder" (compare German *Mord*).

The *-d-* first attested in Middle English *mordre, mourdre, murder, murdre* could have been influenced **by Old French** *murdre*, itself derived from the Germanic noun via **Frankish** *murþra* (compare **Old High German** *murdreo, murdiro*), though the same sound development can be seen with *burden* (from *burthen*). The alternative *murther* (attested up to the 19th century) springs directly from the Old English forms. Middle English *mordre* is a verb from Anglo-Saxon *myrðrian* from Proto-Germanic *murþrijaną*, or, according to the **Oxford English Dictionary**

An eighteenth-century English jurist **William Blackstone** (citing **Edward Coke**), in his **Commentaries on the Laws of England** set out the **common law** definition of murder,

when a person, of sound memory and discretion, unlawfully kills any reasonable creature in being and under the king's peace, with malice aforethought, either express or implied.

Under the common law (law originating from custom and court decisions rather than statutes), murder was an intentional killing that was:

- unlawful (in other words, not legally justified), and

- committed with "malice aforethought."

Malice aforethought doesn't mean that a killer has to have acted out of spite or hate. It exists if a defendant intends to kill someone without legal justification or excuse. In addition, in most states, malice aforethought isn't limited to intentional killings. It can also exist if the killer:

- intentionally inflicts serious bodily harm that causes the victim's death, or

- behaves in a way that shows extreme, reckless disregard for life and results in the victim's death.

In today's society, murder is defined by statute rather than common law. Though today's statutes derive from common law, one has to look to these statutes for important distinctions—like the difference between first- and second-degree murder.

However, murder can become a federal crime if it violates federal laws or occurs on federal land. An example of this would be the murder of a federal judge. Federal murder cases can be either first degree or second degree and may lead to punishments like life imprisonment or the death penalty.

History Of Murder According To Religious Side Of View…

Murder has been traced to our great ancestors **Adam** and **Eve** alongside their children, **Cain** and **Abel**. Genesis 4 in the bible details the **first murder when Cain kills his brother Abel** in a fit of angry jealousy. The Qur'an states that the story of **Cain** and **Abel** was a message for mankind, as it had told them about the consequences of murder and that the killing of a soul would be as if he/she had slain the whole of mankind. But the

Qur'an states that still people rejected the message of the story, and continued to commit grave sins, such as slaying prophets and other righteous people.

Views of Murder according to the torah...

Rashbam, a Hebrew acronym for RAbbi SHmuel Ben Meir, knows that not all the evidence within the Torah supports the distinction that he makes. He attempts to address the problem in that same comment in Exodus:

ומה שכתוב אשר ירצח את רעהו בבלי דעת (דברים ד מב), לפי שמדבר בענין רוצח במזיד לכך הוא אומר ואם רציחה זו בבלי דעת פטור.

When the verse says (Deut. 4:42) "one who unwittingly slew (literally "murdered"; ירצח) a fellow man," since the greater context there deals with premeditated murder, the text says that if such "murdering" (רציחה) takes place unwittingly, then there is no penalty.

Murder and Violent Crimes in Ancient Egypt

Kerry Muhlestein of Brigham Young University wrote: "Rape, domestic violence, and even murder are attested at the village. These illicit acts of violence were viewed, at least by some, in a negative light, for we learn about them in the form of complaints. From three letters of the Late Ramesside era we recover hints of a plot to kill two Medjay apparently in order to keep them from testifying in some manner against the perpetrators. The secrecy of the plot makes it clear that this act would be looked upon most unfavorably, even though people of power were involved. Record s of legal proceedings also hint at violence, such as the acts attempted in connection with the harem conspiracy in the reign of Ramesses. These records may give us a clue as to what Weni, an Old Kingdom official, meant when he enigmatically spoke of hearing a secret matter in the harem, but we cannot know. Similarly, the Persian Period Petition of Petiese outlines a case of murder, giving us a small insight into violent events that must have happened throughout Egyptian history. Royal decrees can provide traces of violent acts among non-royal individuals. [Source: Kerry Muhlestein, Brigham Young University, 2015, UCLA Encyclopedia of Egyptology, 2013 escholarship.org]

"For example, when the 21 st Dynasty Banishment Stela stipulates that murder was worthy of death, we may safely assume that murder was not an unknown act. Similarly, a Demotic literary tale, which culminates in the burning of murderers, implies that such things happened in reality as well, as does a literary tale from the 21 st Dynasty, which recounts the murder of a woman and scattering of her children. Other literary tales portray violence in a negative light, such as when a minor official is portrayed as beating a peasant in such a way that the beating is clearly viewed as unjustifiable and wrong. One of the most profitable sources for learning about violence are oracular texts. For exam ple, we can read of death being decreed by oracle for embezzlers.

"When trials were decided by appeals to oracles, often the deeds of the accused were either written on a text presented to the oracle, or the oracle's decision was writt en down. From these kinds of texts we learn of two boys who were beaten to death and of the execution of their murderers. In another we learn of two men who had been caught in illegal acts trying to murder the man who had discovered them before he could tell anyone. While the official writings of Egypt do not present us with the illicit violence that could be a part of lived experience, such acts become more apparent in their laundry lists.

"Clearly murder, or killing someone who was innocent, was viewed as wrong. Piankhy forbade certain men from entering a temple because they "did a thing which god did not command should be done, they conceived evil in their hearts, even slaying one who was without guilt". "While it is clear that such killing was outside of what the divine and mortal realms sanctioned, it is curious that the punishment, apparently for attempted or at least plotted murder, appears to be so mild. At least in this writing the only punishment listed was a prohibition from entering the temple. This may be due to Piankhy's concentration on purity, for he emphasized that these men had done the killing within the very temple they were forbidden to enter. In a literary narrative, the Tale of the Two Brothers, even a king killing one who was innocent is portrayed negatively. The Myth of the Eye of the Sun more clearly depicts the negative view of those who murdered. In one conversation it is recorded that those who kill should be killed, and that those who go unpunished will never have the blood removed from them and will be punished eventually, even if it is in the next life.

"While in formal complaints or actions, grievous offenses such as adultery were not typically punished by violence, some texts might imply that this could happen on occasion, and a few wisdom texts intimate that it was not unheard of for the wronged spouse to seek illicit retribution."

Murder cases from the Ancient World…

The following ancient murder cases show that things weren't much different in years past. From genocide to intimate killing, this uniquely human act has been with us from the beginning of our existence.

• Georgie of Vindolanda

Vindolanda is an ancient Roman outpost in northern England noted for a set of wooden tablets.

The most important military correspondence ever recovered from the Roman era. But a far grislier discovery was unearthed at this fort near Hadrian's Wall – the 1, 800-year-old remains of a child. Archaeologists named the child Georgie, though the sex is impossible to determine. Because the body was buried in a shallow pit below the barracks rather than cremated (a grave crime under Roman law), archeologists believe the child was murdered. The story gets stranger from there – analysis suggests the victim grew up in the Mediterranean and could have had his or her hands tied at time of death. Was Georgie a slave? A soldier's child? There are still no answers.

- ## Moche Massacre in Peru

The Moche culture existed in what is now modern-day Peru from 100 to 700 CE, prior to the great Incan Empire. It was a largely agricultural society with loose political bonds, yet something very dark occurred in this rustic region. In 1997, archaeologists uncovered a mass grave containing the remains of roughly 100 people. They had been skinned alive, decapitated, drained of their blood, and dumped as food for the birds. All were young men, so the most likely explanation is that they died at the hands of their enemy during battle.

- ## Gallina Genocide in New Mexico

Genocide, the ugliest piece to the human puzzle, has existed since the dawn of time. The Gallina culture lived in what is now New Mexico, from 1100 to 1275 CE, before mysteriously vanishing off the face of the earth. Less than 100 human remains have ever been found from the group and all were victims of violence in some form. One discovery included seven skeletons

<u>in a canyon with their skulls crushed and necks snapped</u>. Of the Gallina dwellings recovered my researchers, many were left in perfect order – save for the ones that were burned with their murdered bodies inside. Was it a form of ethnic cleansing from a neighboring tribe? Many believe that it's plausible.

Seeing all these ugly murder cases from the ancient world let move to the modern world...

Murder in the modern world is the unlawful and intentional killing of one human being by another. The penalty for murder is usually life imprisonment, and in jurisdictions with capital punishment, the death penalty may be imposed. Murder is distinguished from other forms of homicide, such as manslaughter, by the intentions or malice of the perpetrator toward the victim. It is also distinguished from noncriminal homicides, such as the state-sanctioned execution of a criminal convicted of murder and the killing of another in self-defense.

In India according to Section 300 of the Indian Penal Code, 1860, murder is defined as follows:

Murder.--Except in the cases hereinafter excepted, culpable homicide is murder, if the act by which the death is caused is done with the intention of causing death, or- 167 2ndly.-If it is done with the intention of causing such bodily injury as the offender knows to be likely to cause the death of the person to whom the harm is caused. or- 3rdly.-If it is done with the intention of causing bodily injury to any person and the bodily injury intended to be inflicted is sufficient in the ordinary course of nature to cause death, or- 4thly.-If the person committing the act knows that it is so imminently dangerous that it must, in all probability, cause death, or such bodily injury as is likely to cause death, and commits such act without any excuse for incurring the risk of causing death or such injury as aforesaid.[1]

On the other hand, culpable homicide (section 299 of Indian Penal Code, 1860)is defined as

... by causing death of person other than person whose death was intended.--If a person, by doing anything which he intends or knows to be likely to cause death, commits culpable homicide by causing the death of any person, whose death he neither intends nor knows himself to be likely to cause, the culpable homicide committed by the offender is of the description of which it would have been if he had caused the death of the person whose death he intended or knew himself to be likely to cause.

In the United States, the law for **murder** varies by jurisdiction. In most US jurisdictions there is a hierarchy of acts, known collectively as homicide, of which first-degree murder and felony murder are the most serious, followed by second-degree murder and, in a few states, third-degree murder, followed by voluntary manslaughter and involuntary manslaughter which are not as serious, followed by reckless homicide and negligent homicide which are the least serious, and ending finally in justifiable homicide, which is not a crime. However, because there are at least 52 relevant jurisdictions, each with its own criminal code, this is a considerable simplification.[1]

Sentencing also varies widely depending upon the specific murder charge. "Life imprisonment" is a common penalty for first-degree murder, but its meaning varies widely.

Degrees of Murder:

- **First Degree Murder**

California law defines murder as "**unlawful killing of a human, or a fetus, with malice aforethought**'. First-degree murder is the most serious form of murder, and in California, any murders that are committed with intent and premeditation are classified as a first degree murder.

The Elements of First Degree Murder

In order to classify murders in different degrees, criminal law highlights various elements or aspects to take into consideration. A 1st-degree murder must have three key aspects:

- **Intent:** A 1st-degree murder must be committed with some sort of intent to kill the person. The murderer must therefore have attacked or harmed their victim with the purpose of ending their life or doing evil.

- **Deliberation and Premeditation:** Deliberation and premeditation are essential parts of quantifying a first-degree murder. This type of crime must be purposeful and planned out, rather than simply occurring in the heat of the moment.

- **"Malice Aforethought":** "Malice aforethought" is a legal term that basically means that a person who committed the murder did so with an intent to kill and a general disregard for human life.
Enumerated First Degree Murders
In order to simplify the classification of murder charges, many states, including California, have enumerated first-degree murder offenses in order to simplify the conviction process. **In California, examples of these charges include drive-by shootings and gang-related murders.**

First Degree Murder Sentencing and Penalties

As stated earlier, **first-degree murders often have some of the strongest punishments**, and this can be a big difference between 1st and 2nd-degree murders. In California, the punishment for this crime is death or imprisonment in the state prison for life without the possibility of parole, provided certain factors are met.

- **Aggravating Factors**
  There are certain factors that might allow a defendant to be charged with the harshest possible sentence in California. These are called **"aggravating factors"** and include things like:
- The defendant has already committed one or multiple murders in the past
- The victim was a police officer, judge, witness, prosecutor, or juror
- The killing occurred in conjunction with another violent crime like rape

- **The Death Penalty**
  The <u>death penalty</u> may be a possible punishment for those who have been convicted of first-degree murder, and this is the case in California.

- **Life without the Possibility of Parole**
  People with a first-degree murder conviction may also face life in prison without any chance of parole.

- **Lesser Sentences**
  In some situations, those with this type of conviction may face reduced sentences of around 25 years in prison, depending on the precise nature and surrounding factors of the crime.

- ## Second Degree Murder

2nd-degree murder is still a very serious crime but is a step down in severity when compared to the 1st degree. In general terms, a 2nd-degree murder is one that doesn't have any kind of premeditation and may only have been intended to cause harm, rather than death.

In California, the term **second-degree murder is applied to all murders that do not qualify under the category of first-degree murder**. The state defines second-degree murder as any type of **unlawful killing** that is done with malice aforethought but without premeditation.

- ## Intentional Killings Without Premeditation
  One of the defining aspects of a second-degree manslaughter or murder charge is that there isn't any sort of plan or premeditation on behalf of the killer. Even if they intend to kill someone at the moment of the crime, it may simply occur in the heat of the moment and isn't something that they planned out in advance.

- ## Intent to Cause Only Serious Bodily Harm
  This is another factor that might define second-degree murder. The defendant might not have actually intended to kill their victim. Instead, they may have only had the intent to cause serious bodily harm.

- ## Extreme Indifference to Human Life
  Another type of second-degree murder is when a victim dies because the defendant showed an extreme level of indifference for their life.

- ## Felony Murder
  Felony murder is when someone is killed during the course of a

felony, like a robbery. This can be classed as both first-degree and second-degree murder in California.

Second Degree Murder Penalties and Sentencing
The sentencing for second-degree murders can vary from **15 years to life in prison in California**.

- **Aggravating and Mitigating Factors for Second Degree Murder**
  A range of aggravating and mitigating factors can come into play during sentencing. Aggravating factors like **cruel or brutal acts and previous convictions could increase the severity of the sentence**. Mitigating factors like **mental illness or a troubled childhood can reduce the severity of the sentence.**

- **Second Degree Murder Sentencing Procedure**
  The **procedure for sentencing** in this kind of crime will depend on **the location, the nature of the crime, and other factors**. Usually, a court hearing will be held to find out more about the case and weigh up the factors, before sentencing is issued.

  - **Third-Degree Murder**
  There is no such thing as third-degree murder under California law. California only recognizes three types of murder charges: first degree, second degree, and capital murder. **The idea of a third-degree murder charge only exists in three states: Florida, Pennsylvania, and Minnesota.**
  What Is the Difference Between Third-Degree Murder and Manslaughter?
  On the face of it, **3rd-degree murder and manslaughter are very similar**, but the states in which a **third-degree murder**

charge can apply differentiate between them in different ways.

For example, in Minnesota, someone must act with disregard for human life and a depraved mind to be charged with 3rd-degree murder, but will only face manslaughter charges if they were aware of the risks to another life but went ahead with their actions anyway, such as vehicular manslaughter or <u>driving under the influence – causing death</u> to another person.

Penalties for Third Degree Murder

The penalties for this crime vary based on location. **In Florida, the penalty can be up to 15 years imprisonment and fines of up to $10,000**. In **Minnesota, defendants can be sentenced to 25 years behind bars and $40,000 fines**. In **Pennsylvania, the maximum sentence is 40 years in prison**, and the penalties for this crime are similar to penalties for attempted murder or voluntary manslaughter.

How Do Murderers Behave?

Traits common to some serial murderers, including **sensation seeking, a lack of remorse or guilt, impulsivity, the need for control, and predatory behavior**. These traits and behaviors are consistent with the psychopathic personality disorder. Serial killers characteristically lack empathy for others, coupled with an apparent absence of guilt about their actions. At the same time, many can be superficially charming, allowing them to lure potential victims into their web of destruction. Murderers have been diagnosed with psychological disorders such as **antisocial personality disorder or other personality disturbances, psychological stressors,**

various types of childhood trauma, and drug and alcohol abuse problems.

Dating back to ancient times, serial murderers have been chronicled around the world. In 19th century Europe, Dr. Richard von Krafft-Ebing conducted some of the first documented research on violent, sexual offenders and the crimes they committed. Best known for his 1886 textbook **Psychopathia Sexualis,**Dr. Kraft-Ebing described numerous case studies of sexual homicide, serial murder, and other areas of sexual proclivity.

Serial murder is a relatively rare event, estimated to comprise less than one percent of all murders committed in any given year. However, there is a macabre interest in the topic that far exceeds its scope and has generated countless articles, books, and movies. This broad-based public fascination began in the late 1880s, after a series of unsolved prostitute murders occurred in the Whitechapel area of London. These murders were committed by an unknown individual who named himself "Jack the Ripper" and sent letters to the police claiming to be the killer.

Dear Boss
I keep on hearing the police have caught me but they wont fix me just yet. I have laughed when they look so clever and talk about being on the right track. That joke about Leather Apron gave me real fits. I am down on whores and I shant quit ripping them till I do get buckled. Grand work the last job was. I gave the lady no time to squeal. How can they catch me now. I love my work and want to start again. You will soon hear of me with my funny little games. I saved some of the proper red stuff in a ginger beer bottle over the last job to write with but it went thick like glue and I cant use it. Red ink is fit enough I hope ha. ha. The next job I do I shall clip the ladys ears off and send to the police officers just for jolly wouldn't you. Keep this letter back till I do a bit more work, then give it out straight. My knife's so nice and sharp I want to get to work right away if I get a chance. Good luck.
Yours truly
Jack the Ripper

These murders and the nom de guerre "Jack the Ripper" have become synonymous with serial murder. This case spawned many legends concerning serial murder and the killers who commit it. In the 1970s and 1980s serial murder cases such as the Green River Killer, Ted Bundy, and BTK sparked a renewed public interest in serial murder, which blossomed in the 1990s after the release of films such as **Silence of the Lambs**.

Much of the general public's knowledge concerning serial murder is a product of Hollywood productions. Story lines are created to heighten the interest of audiences, rather than to accurately portray serial murder. By focusing on the atrocities inflicted on victims by "deranged" offenders, the public is captivated by the criminals and their crimes. This only lends more confusion to the true dynamics of serial murder.

Law enforcement professionals are subject to the same misinformation from a different source: the use of anecdotal information. Professionals involved in serial murder cases, such as investigators, prosecutors, and pathologists may have limited exposure to serial murder. Their experience may be based upon a single murder series, and the factors in that case are extrapolated to other serial murders. As a result, certain stereotypes and misconceptions take root regarding the nature of serial murder and the characteristics of serial killers.

A growing trend that compounds the fallacies surrounding serial murder is the talking heads phenomenon. Given creditability by the media, these self-proclaimed authorities profess to have an expertise in serial murder. They appear frequently on television and in the print media and speculate on the motive for the murders and the characteristics of the possible offender, without being privy to the facts of the investigation. Unfortunately, inappropriate comments may perpetuate misperceptions concerning serial murder and impair law enforcement's investigative efforts. It was decided by a majority of the attendees to issue a formal statement of position regarding the media's use of these types of individuals.

Serial killers are all dysfunctional loners.

The majority of serial killers are not reclusive, social misfits who live alone. They are not monsters and may not appear strange. Many serial killers hide in plain sight within their communities. Serial murderers often have families and homes, are gainfully employed, and appear to be normal members of the community. Because many serial murderers can blend in so effortlessly, they are oftentimes overlooked by law enforcement and the public.

• Robert Yates killed seventeen prostitutes in the Spokane, Washington area, during the 1990s. He was married with five children, lived in a middle class neighborhood, and was a decorated U.S. Army National Guard helicopter pilot. During the time period of the murders, Yates routinely patronized prostitutes, and several of his victims knew each other. Yates buried one of his victims in his yard, beneath his bedroom window. Yates was eventually arrested and pled guilty to thirteen of the murders.

• The Green River Killer, Gary Ridgeway, confessed to killing 48 women over a twenty-year time period in the Seattle, Washington area. He had been married three times and was still married at the time of his arrest. He was employed as a truck painter for thirty-two years. He attended church regularly, read the Bible at home and at work, and talked about religion with co-workers. Ridgeway also frequently picked up prostitutes and had sex with them throughout the time period in which he was killing.

• The BTK killer, Dennis Rader, killed ten victims in and around Wichita, Kansas. He sent sixteen written communications to the news media over a thirty-year period, taunting the police and the public. He was married with two children, was a Boy Scout leader, served honorably in the U.S. Air Force, was employed as a local government official, and was president of his church.

Serial killers are only motivated by sex.

All serial murders are not sexually-based. There are many other motivations for serial murders including anger, thrill, financial gain, and attention seeking.

• In the Washington, D.C. area serial sniper case, John Allen Muhammad, a former U.S. Army Staff Sergeant, and Lee Boyd Malvo killed primarily for anger and thrill motivations. They were able to terrorize the greater Washington, D.C. metro area for three weeks, shooting 13 victims, killing 10 of them. They communicated with the police by leaving notes, and they attempted to extort money to stop the shootings. They are suspected in a number of other shootings in seven other states.

• Dr. Michael Swango, a former U.S. Marine, ambulance worker, and physician, was a health care employee. He was convicted of only four murders in New York and Ohio, although he is suspected of having poisoned and killed 35 to 50 people throughout the United States and on the continent of Africa. Swango's motivation for the killings was intrinsic and never fully identified. Interestingly, Swango kept a scrap book filled with newspaper and magazine clippings about natural disasters, in which many people were killed.

• Paul Reid killed at least seven people during fast food restaurant robberies in Tennessee. After gaining control of the victims, he either stabbed or shot them. The motivation for the murders was primarily witness elimination. Reid's purpose in committing the robberies was financial gain, and some of the ill-gotten gains were used to purchase a car.

Serial killers cannot stop killing.

It has been widely believed that once serial killers start killing, they cannot stop. There are, however, some serial killers who stop murdering altogether before being caught. In these instances, there are events or circumstances in offenders' lives that inhibit them from pursuing more victims. These can include increased participation in family activities, sexual substitution, and other diversions.

• BTK killer, Dennis Rader, murdered ten victims from 1974 to 1991. He did not kill any other victims prior to being captured in 2005. During interviews conducted by law enforcement, Rader admitted to engaging in auto-erotic activities as a substitute for his killings.

• Jeffrey Gorton killed his first victim in 1986 and his next victim in 1991. He did not kill another victim and was captured in 2002. Gorton engaged in cross-dressing and masturbatory activities, as well as consensual sex with his wife in the interim.

All Serial killers are insane or are evil geniuses.

Another myth that exists is that serial killers have either a debilitating mental condition, or they are extremely clever and intelligent.

As a group, serial killers suffer from a variety of personality disorders, including psychopathy, anti-social personality, and others. Most, however, are not adjudicated as insane under the law.

The media has created a number of fictional serial killer "geniuses", who outsmart law enforcement at every turn. Like other populations, however, serial killers range in intelligence from borderline to above average levels.

Serial killers want to get caught.

Offenders committing a crime for the first time are inexperienced. They gain experience and confidence with each new offense, eventually succeeding with few mistakes or problems.

While most serial killers plan their offenses more thoroughly than other criminals, the learning curve is still very steep. They must select, target, approach, control, and dispose of their victims. The logistics involved in committing a murder and disposing of the body can become very complex, especially when there are multiple sites involved.

As serial killers continue to offend without being captured, they can become empowered, feeling they will never be identified. As the series continues, the killers may begin to take shortcuts when committing their crimes. This often causes the killers to take more chances, leading to identification by law enforcement. It is not that serial killers want to get caught; they feel that they can't get caught.

Who are the Murderers?

A murderer is a person who kills deliberately and without justification.

In some instances, killing a person is considered a just or valid action — in a war, a soldier who kills another soldier is not considered to be a murderer, and people who kill in self-defense, to save themselves, are also not murderers. Killing out of anger or for money or revenge is murder, and anyone who does it is a murderer.

This list below shows all known serial killers from the 20th century to present day by number of victims, then possible victims, then date. In many cases, the exact number of victims assigned to a serial killer is not known, and even if that person is convicted of a few, there can be the possibility that they killed many more.

Ahmad Suradji	Indonesia	1986–1997	42	70–80+	Suradji was convicted of strangling at least 42 women and girls in a series of ritual slayings he believed would give him magical powers. He was executed by firing squad in 2008.[32]
Alexander Pichushkin	Russia	1992–2006	49	60	Pichushkin was also known as the "Chessboard Killer". He was convicted of murdering 49 victims, and suspected of killing 60. He claimed to have murdered 62 people, because he did not know that two of his victims had survived; he stated that his goal was becoming Russia's most prolific serial killer.[29] He was sentenced to life imprisonment.
Ali Asghar Borujerdi	Ottoman Empire Iraq Iran	1907–1934	33	33	Known as "Asghar the Murderer". Borujerdi killed 33 young adults in Iraq and Iran. He was executed by hanging in 1934.[43]
Anatoly Onoprienko	Soviet Union Ukraine	1989–1996	52	52+	Known as "The Beast of Ukraine", "The Terminator", and "Citizen O". Onoprienko was convicted of the murders of nine people in 1989, and 43 people in 1995–1996. He

					travelled throughout Europe illegally from 1990 to 1995; whether he killed during this time is unknown. He was sentenced to death, and was later commuted to imprisonment for life. He died from heart failure in 2013.[23]
Andrei Chikatilo	Soviet Union	1978–1990	53	56	Known as "The Butcher of Rostov", "The Red Ripper" or "The Rostov Ripper". Chikatilo was convicted of the murder of 53 women and children between 1978 and 1990. One man was previously convicted and executed for his first murder. Chikatilo was executed by gunshot in 1994.[23]
Clementine Barnabet	United States	1911	35	35	Barnebet was an axe murdering voodoo priestess who murdered African-American families at nighttime.[41] She was released in 1923.
Daniel Camargo Barbosa	Colombia Ecuador Brazil (alleged)[13]	1974–1986	72	180[13]	Child and woman murderer, believed to have possibly raped and killed over 150 victims, primarily targeting female children, as they were more likely to be virgins. Confessed to killing 72 victims. He strangled young girls in Colombia and was arrested, but he escaped from prison, and started killing in Ecuador. He was rearrested in 1986, and was allegedly incarcerated in the same Ecuadorian prison as 300+ serial killer Pedro López.[citation needed] Camargo was killed in jail by the nephew of one of his victims.[13][14]
Fernando Hernández Leyva	Mexico	1982–1999	33	137	Hernández Leyva confessed to 100 murders and six kidnappings at the time of his arrest in 1999 (he had been arrested previously in 1982 and 1986, the second time for murder, but escaped from prison), but later retracted, and claimed that he had been beaten by the police and his family threatened in order to

Name	Country	Years active	Proven victims	Possible victims	Notes
					force him to confess. He was accused of as many as 137 murders in five southern Mexican states, was convicted of 33 murders, and was sentenced to 50 years in prison. He tried unsuccessfully to commit suicide in prison. If his claim of 100+ victims were true, then Leyva would be Mexico's most prolific documented serial killer.[44]
Florisvaldo de Oliveira	Brazil	1982–1983	50	50+	Known as "Cabo Bruno"; de Oliveira was a former police officer and vigilante who murdered criminals in the outskirts of São Paulo. He was murdered by unknown assailants in 2012.[26]
Gary Ridgway	United States	1982–2000	49	71–90+	Ridgway was a truck painter who confessed to killing 71 women. He was also known as The "Green River Killer". He almost exclusively targeted sex workers from Seattle. Ridgway was suspected of killing over 90 victims; he confessed to 71, and was convicted of 49.[27] He was sentenced to life without parole.[28]
Gennady Mikhasevich	Soviet Union	1971–1985	36	43–55+	Mikhasevich killed women by strangling them. Besides killing, he also robbed his victims of money and valuable items (that he would sometimes give to his wife as a gift). He was executed by firing squad in 1987.[36]
Hadj Mohammed Mesfewi	Morocco	1906 and earlier	36	36+	Known as "Marrakesh Arch-Killer"; Mesfewi drugged, mutilated and murdered women; he was executed by immurement (walling) in 1906.
Ivan Maleshoff	Soviet Union	1934–1935	50	50	Known as, "Bluebeard of Kharkiv"; Ivan Stepanovich Maleshoff was an electrical engineer, and prolific albeit little known Soviet serial killer. He is purported to

					have killed 20 women in Kharkiv over a period of several months in 1935 with a knife, leaving behind little clues as to his identity, other than taunting letters to police. Reportedly, apprehended by authorities as he attempted to kill his next victim, completely unaware he had been tailed after seen fleeing arrest by an undercover female officer earlier in the day. Prior to his execution, he confessed to an additional 30 murders in nearby Kyiv in 1934. He was convicted and executed in 1935 by firing squad at the age of 40.[24][25]
Javed Iqbal	☪ Pakistan	1998–1999	100	100	Child-murderer and rapist, known as "Kukri", Iqbal murdered 100 street children by strangling them and covering up his crimes by dissolving the bodies with acid. He was arrested in 1999 after sending a letter to a newspaper, and was set to be executed in the manner described by the judge who stated, "You will be strangled to death in front of the parents whose children you killed, Your body will then be cut into 100 pieces and put in acid, the same way you killed the children."[8] However, he died in custody before he could be executed.[9]
John Wayne Gacy	▤ United States	1972–1978	33	34-45+	Gacy is known to have murdered a minimum of 33 teenage boys and young men between 1972 and 1978, 26 of whom he buried in the crawl space of his Chicago home. He was known as the "Killer Clown", due to the fact he often entertained children at social events dressed in a self devised clown costume. Executed by lethal injection in 1994.[42]
Kampatimar Shankariya	▬ India	1977–1978	70	70+	Shankariya was an Indian serial killer who used a hammer to kill over 70 men and women between 1978 and 1979. He was hanged in 1979; his last words were, "I have

					murdered in vain", he declared. "Nobody should become like me."[16][17][18][19]
Vasili Komaroff	Soviet Union	1921–1923	33	33	Known as "The Wolf of Moscow"; Komaroff was a horse trader who killed 33 men. He was executed by firing squad in 1923.
Pedro López	Colombia Peru Ecuador	1969–1980	110	300+	Child-murderer and rapist, known as "The Monster of the Andes". López targeted young girls, between the ages of eight and twelve. Arrested in 1980 and convicted in 1983 of killing three young girls, but claimed to have killed hundreds. Despite being believed to be one of the most prolific serial killers of the twentieth century, he was released in the late 1990s.[7]
Luis Garavito	Colombia Ecuador[3] Venezuela[3]	1992–1999[3]	193	193–300+	Child-murderer, torture-killer, and rapist known as *La Bestia* ("The Beast"). Garavito confessed to killing 140 boys between six and sixteen years old, from October 1992 to April 1999 in Colombia and neighboring countries.[3] He is suspected of murdering over 300 victims, mostly street children. Garavito was originally sentenced to 1,853 years in prison, but this was later reduced to 22 years, after he led police to many of the bodies of his victims.[4][5] He is scheduled to become eligible for parole in 2023.[6]
Mikhail Popkov	Russia	1992–2010	78	83+	Serial rapist-killer nicknamed "The Werewolf", who was active for two decades in Angarsk, Irkutsk and Vladivostok. After being convicted of 22 murders in 2015, he confessed to an additional 59 murders, of which he was convicted of 56 in 2018.[10][11] In July 2020, Popkov confessed to more killings, bringing the total number of admitted victims to 83.[12] He was sentenced

					to life.
Mohammed Bijeh	Iran	2004	43	43	Bijeh raped and killed at least 41 male children and teenagers. He was nicknamed the "Tehran Desert Vampire". Bijeh was convicted and executed after being lashed in front of a crowd in 2005.[31]
Moses Sithole	South Africa	1994–1995	38	76	Known as South Africa's Ted Bundy. Sithole preyed on unemployed women, posing as a businessman and luring his victims with the prospects of a job, before leading them to an isolated place, where he raped, tortured, and murdered them. He was sentenced to 2,410 years imprisonment, with a non-parole period of 930 years.[34]
Pedro Rodrigues Filho	Brazil	1967–2003	71	100+	Rodrigues Filho claimed to have killed over 100 victims, 47 of them inmates. He also killed his father and ate a piece of his heart. He killed his first two victims at the age of 14. He was first arrested in 1973; he was convicted and sentenced to 128 years, but the maximum one can serve in Brazil is 30 years.[15] He was released in 2018.

Murder is wrong morally

Human murder shit all the time. But when we kill someone without reason, it becomes a crime. It isn't right to kill someone without cause.

In the Quran, the preceding verse of the Qur'an (Maida 5:32), God Almighty commands the Prophet "Narrate to them (O Messenger) in truth the exemplary experience of the two sons of

Adam…" and draws attention to the first murder committed on the earth.

THE FIRST MURDER AND THE MASTER OF MURDERERS

Most Qur'anic interpreters say that the two sons of Adam are Cain and Abel and they give detailed information about the lives of these two brothers. Actually, their names are not mentioned in the Qur'an; but in the ancient scriptures and narrations the names of Adam's sons are mentioned as Cain and Abel. It is for this reason that Muslim scholars have not found anything wrong in referring to the characters involved in the event by these names. At the same time, some have interpreted the "two sons of Adam" to be just two men from the Children of Israel. In truth, one doesn't have to know their names in order to learn a lesson from the parable. What matters is the fact that this event did happen and the expression "in truth" mentioned in the verse shows that this is not a myth, but a true story.

As narrated in the Qur'an, they both offered a sacrifice to God; but only one of these was accepted. The brother whose sacrifice was not accepted told the other "I will surely kill you." Despite the fact that killing a person, particularly killing one's own brother, is a great transgression, the murderer, who had lost control due to jealousy, shed the blood of his innocent brother; this brother did not even attempt to struggle against his brother, and he was only a good-intentioned companion.

KILLING UNJUSTLY AND RETALIATION

The murder stated in the verse as equal to killing all of mankind is limited to "killing an innocent person who did not cause disorder or corruption on the earth." This means that if a person sheds the blood of innocent people, there can be retaliation and that killer can face a penalty similar to his own crime. If such a person causes disorder on the earth and therefore causes people to die, if the killings follow one upon another without the killer thinking why they had taken a life and if the victims do not know why they are being killed-as is happening in some parts of the world today-the criminal or the group of criminals who cause such anarchy can be executed. The people who start wars against God and His Messenger, who cause disorder on the earth, who habitually transgress against people's lives, properties, and chastity, thereby disturbing the order of society, corrupting the generation, should be executed or sent into exile in accordance with the gravity of their crime.

To End It All...

In the well-known story of Cain and Abel, the first man born on the earth also becomes the first murderer. A few points in this account are significant:

- Cain killed Abel after a quarrel over a sacrifice to <u>God</u>. Cain brought a sacrifice, but God would not accept it because it did not meet His standards. While Abel's offering showed his complete submission to God, Cain's hints at grudging worship of God - and that done in his own way.
- Becoming angry and sullen over his rejection, he quarreled with and killed his brother. Then, he lied to God's face! He had no fear of God or the consequences of sin.
- Cain's retort to God's inquiry as to Abel's whereabouts is also significant: "Am I my brother's keeper?" Cain's attitude of indifference toward his fellow man greatly influenced later generations.
- Coupled with his entirely selfish attitude, Cain tried to take advantage even of God's curse upon him. Using a "woe is me" ploy, he "convinced" God to guard his life from anyone avenging Abel's murder.

www.ingramcontent.com/pod-product-compliance
Lightning Source LLC
Chambersburg PA
CBHW080923160726
48000CB00009B/3108